M000281349

HAPPY BIRTHDAY TO YOU ON YOUR 50TH BIRTHDAY!

Sample Preview

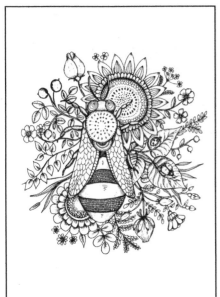

ArtTherapyColoring.com

Sample Preview

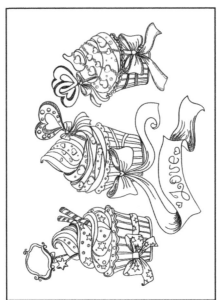

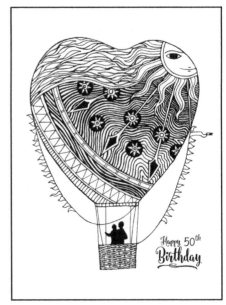

Happy Birthday!

HAPPY
BIRTHDAY!

Happy Birthday

Happy 50th Birthday

Happy Birthday!

Happy Birthday!

HAPPY BIRTHDAY!

Happy Birthday!

Happy Birthday!

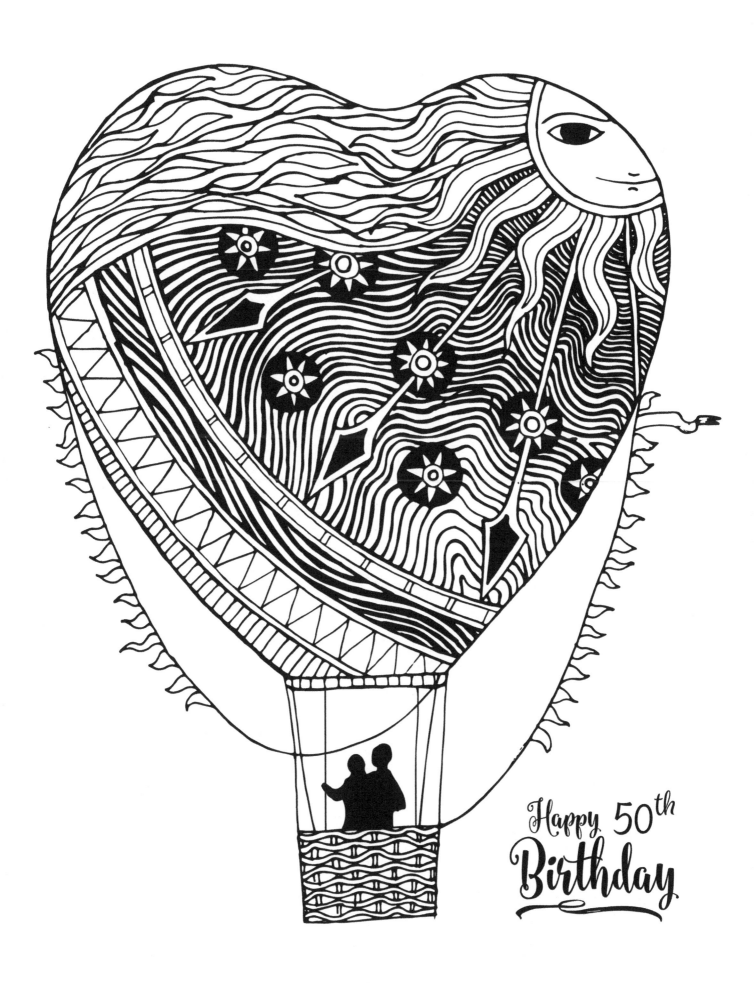

Happy 50th Birthday

Popular Coloring Books

Coloring Books for Adults:

- Zombie Coloring Book: Black Background
- Butterfly Coloring Book For Adults: Black Background
- Tattoo Coloring Book: Black Background
- Coloring Books for Adults Relaxation: Native American Inspired Designs
- Fishing Coloring Book for Adults: Black Background

Coloring Books for Men:

- Coloring Book for Men: Anti-Stress Designs Vol 1
- Coloring Book For Men: Fishing Designs
- Coloring Book For Men: Tattoo Designs
- Coloring Books for Men: Hunting
- Coloring Book For Men: Biker Designs

Coloring Books for Seniors:

- Coloring Book For Seniors: Nature Designs Vol 1
- Coloring Book For Seniors: Anti-Stress Designs Vol 1
- Coloring Books for Seniors: Relaxing Designs
- Coloring Book For Seniors: Floral Designs Vol 1
- Coloring Book For Seniors: Ocean Designs Vol 1

Coloring Books for Teens:

- Coloring Books For Teens: Ocean Designs
- Coloring Books For Teens: Wolves & More
- Teen Inspirational Coloring Books
- Coloring Book for Teens: Anti-Stress Designs Vol 1
- Coloring Books for Teen Girls Vol 1

Coloring Books for Kids:

- Horse Coloring Book For Girls
- Coloring Books For Boys: Sharks
- Coloring Books for Boys: Animal Designs
- Unicorn Coloring Book for Girls
- Detailed Coloring Books For Kids

Test Your Colors

Happy Birthday To You On Your 50th Birthday

Published by:
Art Therapy Coloring
www.arttherapycoloring.com

Copyright © 2018 by Art Therapy Coloring
All Rights Reserved

Images Under License From Shutterstock

Made in the USA
Middletown, DE
02 April 2020

87607905R00051